An Old Oak

An Old Oak

*Collection of Poems
and Quotes*

Rebecca Holland Pilgrim

An Old Oak

As one Looks out across an open field as far as the eye can see… amazing green grass with sunflowers leaning forward and smiling up at me. Standing in the center of this paradise is a solitary old Oak. A strong mighty oak with its branches reaching far and wide, its roots planted deep within the dark soil of the earth.

A mighty old oak tree stands tall reaching upward to the sky. The old oak stands alone, unmoving, solid, and proud, reminds one of a man, an unforgettable man. He is as the old oak, solid, unmoving, and proud, reaching out beyond the fields with his roots planted deep in the rich dark soil of the earth, standing alone to make America great AGAIN.

A man with an exterior as coarse as an old oak's bark, rigid and stout. He has weathered many storms, suffered, sacrificed and lost many branches along the way, but still at the end of the day… an Old Oak stands tall, solid, and proud.

We remember with gleeful pleasure those shared twits of daring honesty. Like a love to a lover one sighs with satisfaction, Like the musician whose lyrics have taken the town, the golfer whose life goal of hole-in-one has come true, and that final victory lap, took the flag. As the morning dawn with its promise of a new day of sunshine turns into dark skies full of rain clouds and raging winds destined to destroy the old Oak has remained steady and true.

The old Oak with its graying leaves blowing in the wind while whipping up old stories of days gone by. The sounds seem to come alive as the approaching storm with its drenching rains and hails of disloyalties move ever so closer. Yet, the winds of defeat will not sound true and a yearning for hope and real change cries out to be heard. While there are those that feel threatened one knows with certainty all is safe nestled here beneath the mighty old oak.

Yes, Safe in the knowledge that when the hard cover of the old oak chips and falls, little by little, piece by piece, naked and exposed for the entire world to see, even then the mighty old oak is not afraid to fight for country or thee. Even now, through the eye of the storm one can almost feel the warmth of a true beating heart, feel the softness of a soothing hand, the strength of the mighty Oak. We know the best of the old Oak is yet to come.

An old oak solid, enduring, and forever proud I think of you with longing and a smile.

Revised for "The Donald" the greatest president of my lifetime.

An old Oak

The original, written for Woodside

As I look out across an open field as far as the eye can see ... amazing green grass with sunflowers leaning forward smiling at the sun. In the center of this sunny paradise standing alone is an old oak. A mighty oak with its branches reaching far and wide, its roots planted deep within the dark soil of the earth.

A mighty oak tree standing tall almost reaching to the sky.

The old oak stands alone, unmoving, solid and grand. It reminds one of a man, an unforgettable man. He is... as the old oak, solid, unmoving and proud. He never reaches out beyond his fields, his roots planted solid and deep within his familiar ground.

A man with an exterior as coarse as the old oak's bark, ridged, and stout. He has weathered many storms, suffered and lost many branches along the way but, still at the end of day, he stands solid and proud. A magnificent old oak.

Every now and then the memories take one back to those cherished moments, precious times when the hard bark of the old oak's cover would chip and fall, piece by piece, exposing the kind gentle interior. The best of the old oak would come shining through. Those shared moments of unguarded openness were beautiful, beautiful as a morning dawn with the promise of a new day full of sunshine.

One must hold close to the heart the sweetness of the nights, they were calm and soothing as rainfall on a tin roof, while others were windy with raw passion. Those nights easily remain in one's thoughts... fresh and satisfying as resting under the shade of an old oak on a hot summer day. One never wants to leave that wonderful place...beneath the old oak.

An old oak, strong, solid, enduring and forever proud. I will always think of you with longing and a smile.

May, 1994

Have You

Have you ever heard the wind whispering in the pines?
Have you ever seen the sun when it failed to shine?
Have you ever seen a blue sky turn orange at the end of the day?
Have you ever seen a girl who did not want to play?
Have you ever kissed a boy and knew right away?
Have you ever loved someone whose heart was broken?
Have you ever forgotten the pain of rejection?
Have you ever pretended it was him while kissing another?
Have you ever walked down death row with twenty minutes left to
    live?
Have you ever been strapped to the chair they call death?
Have you ever been spared by one single breath?
Have you ever ...

1970

A Kind of Girl

A baby girl.

A daughter of a mother of nine children.

A daughter afraid of her drunkard father.

A baby girl who knew little of love or the feelings of being loved.

A girl who grew up fast and learned to understand the meaning of emotional neglect.

A rebel girl.

A rebel girl who followed alongside her older sister to become a reckless defiant teen.

A stubborn girl who knew nothing of childbirth.

A rebellious teenage mother one hot August evening.

A tiny hand with the bluest eyes, with the sweetest red face was placed in the girl's arms.

A child-mother alone.

A woman of sixteen, the girl who vows to escape poverty and her life of ignorance.

A determination to become a kind of girl, like no other.

A child, girl, teen, woman, a liar of life.

A kind of girl who holds truths close inside.

A protector from the cruelties of life and the stigma of societies wrath.

A kind of GIRL ... that no one sees but me.

1971

Arms of loneliness

In a world filled with sorrow
with no hope for tomorrow
with the arms of loneliness holding me tight
No future do I see, for these four cold walls
keep me from thee
with the arms of loneliness holding me tight.
Cold gray walls the misery you bring
keep me lingering on and on.
In a cell of living hell
where I'd gladly welcome death
with the arms of loneliness holding me tight
Cold gray walls you keep my love from me
both day and night
destroying my dreams of a happy life.
please release me
For if you cannot,
I will die
with the
arms of loneliness holding me tight.

1975

Yesterday

Yesterday, my love …I slipped and called you darling.
I saw her look at you and wonder why.
If I've caused one tear to fall or darkened your new dream
remember, I innocently forgot you are not mine.
Please forgive me for calling you darling
it's difficult to control the things I say or do.
My only excuse is…. I simply cannot stop myself from loving you.
Its true…

1976

"Wrong love"

To all those who love even when society objects.

They say it is wrong to love you the way that I do. But, I can't ignore this feeling of love I have for you.

So should I love you openly the way my heart desires or should I love you secretly always on the sly?

I'm not asking for advice. I'm just talking to my mind, trying to ease this ache I feel inside. True love you can't forget no matter how you try and talking to your conscience won't ease one's aching mind.

I say, let this love that we are living linger on and on, let the gossip fans talk about us long after we are gone. Let us leave our mark on gossip fans and the world to see, that the "wrong affair" that we shared was the best in all history!

The wrong affair that we shared was the best thing that ever happened to me.

1977

Dedicated to my sister whose interracial marriage was forbidden in our family; yet, she loved, married, and for a time was happy.

Unhappiness

No one ever explained to me that unhappiness feels so much like fear, the sensation of being afraid. The heart fluttering in ones' chest as if running a race, the restless yawning and constant tapping of the foot... the gentle pressure upon the chest... pain .... At times unhappiness feels like being mildly intoxicated without the satisfaction or the jubilation and delight of drunkenness.

In the state of unhappiness one may find it hard to comprehend or focus on what others are saying or perhaps simply elect not to pay attention. One's vision appears cloudy, the body trapped in the fogginess of needing and wanting others around. Yet, totally uninterested in what they have to say, not hearing, and not even pretending to care. Nonetheless, dreading the moment of being total alone.

One may never truly experience the real feelings of happiness or unhappiness, only experiencing brief moments that are pleasurable. The thrill of the moment that quickly passes out of one's mind. Understanding happiness is simply absent.

While there are those who may believe or come to believe that their daily life of routine eating, sleeping, working, and occasional sex is happiness. In truth, if expressed honestly, the reality of happiness is lost in longing for more and the demands of society to have more.

The cold truth of real happiness is the beginning of a long separation from contentment, desires and heart felt emotions. One is confined inside this invisible aura of...searching for.... longing for....and most often never finding.

In the end the search and pursuit of happiness is over and there is death and ...for those left behind

Unhappiness again.

1978

Home of the Blues

Just around the corner, there is heartache down the street that losers
walk. If you wade through the teardrops, you will find me at
the home of the blues.

I walk and cry while my heart keeps perfect rhythm with the drag
of my shoes. The sun never shines through the cloudy windows
of my mine, its darkness at the home of the blues.

Oh, but the home of the blues is full of the sweetest memories,
memories so sweet I could laugh, cry, and running around
naked until I die.

The home of the blues calls out to me, calling your name out loud,
reminding me of all the dreams we had. I suppose I should stop
all the dreariness and paint these dull walls bright red.

If you lose your lover and it seems there is no good way to go, come
along with me. Misery loves company—you'll be welcome here
at the home of the blues.

1979

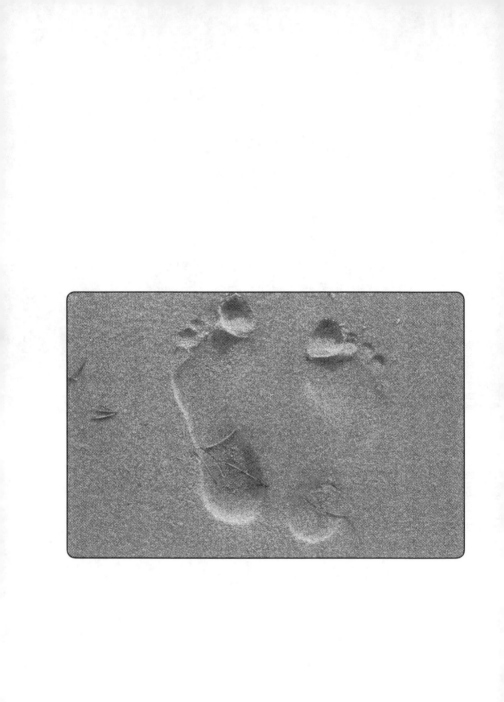

Lonely Am I

To my soon to be ex..Stan

Lonely am I in the heat of the day
    when all is sunny and gay.
Lonely am I when the sky is clear and blue
    but, I don't have you.
Lonely am I when your memory is near,
    when it's your voice I long to hear.
Lonely am I when the music plays soft and slow,
    and the words to the melody are saying *I love you so.*
Lonely am I when I think of our happier days
    when we were in love, full of life, and ready to play.
Lonely am I when I see lovers laugh, sing, and dance
    knowing our life together has gone away.
Lonely and am I when memories of you and her flood my thoughts
    And torture my heart.
Lonely am I. Lonely am I, Lonely am I this day.

1981

Everyone

Everyone is living in a world they want to change

Everyone is loving, but it all seems in vain.

Everyone is believing in the truth when they know the words are rotten lies.

Everyone is singing love songs when everyone knows love songs make you cry.

Everyone is talking, still, they need someone to tell them what to do.

Everyone has a gun in one hand and a crutch in the other.

Everyone wants to kill or lean on their brother.

Everyone is wondering whose to blame.

Everyone complaining about this shameful state that doesn't seem to change.

Everyone living in a world they want to change.

1981

No Words Spoken

On meeting Joey, my husband

I saw you peek you head around the umpire box looking my way.

With no words spoken, I saw a twinkle in your eyes, a softness and warmth in your face. I saw hidden there in your beautiful smile a longing for oneness with me.

With no words spoken, your eyes moved over me and I instantly recognized that certain look, a look one shares with a lover.

With no words spoken, I felt an intense need in your stare, an expression of passionate desire. Only you knew that we would become lovers, one day.

With no words spoken, something in your gentle glance touched me and knew me. Your tender manner made me want you too.

With no words spoken, I returned your smile and walked away….. until another day

1982

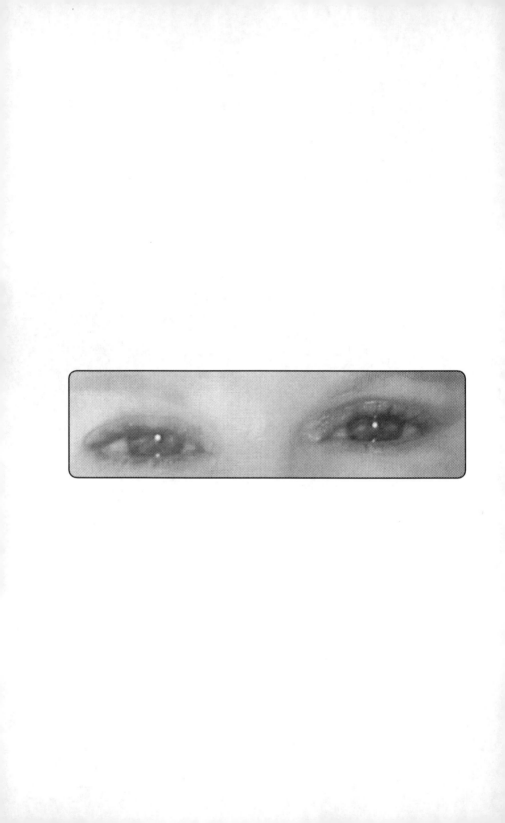

Intuition

Discovering husband sleeping with neighbor

Let your intuition guide you. Trust in those undeniable instincts. Believe strongly, listen quietly, and stay silent. Silence is golden. Do not allow groundless stories to penetrate the layers of your brain and your instinctive thoughts.

Have faith in what is clearly true. Do not deny your gut feelings. Run, walk, or escape to wherever those feelings lead you. Understand in your heart and soul whatever you find was meant to be found.

Discover peace, freedom, and comfort in knowing what you thought and believed to be true, is true. In fact, your intuition is a certainty that must never be ignored.

Independence and truth will be your friend in the end. Grow in faith, develop a plan, and believe in your innate knowing.

Intuition will always ring true and life will begin anew

1983

I Miss You

I miss you, we talked everyday... We kissed and held each other every night.... it's hard to keep from crying... it's even harder to sleep without you here by my side. I must constantly remind myself why you are not here. What countless pain and anguish you have caused me through the years.

I remind myself to breath and shout to myself that today can only get better.

That soon you will be as a flicker is to the flame...almost out! But not today ....today, you are here hurting my chest... pounding my brain... starving my heart.

You took from me what made me feel alive... you took from us a love like no other...You betrayed... you betrayed me and you betrayed yourself.

I realize there is not much I can do, we are apart. you have gone away.

I ... I need to stay focused...continue to forcefully swallow and breath...shake this unhealthy emotion. Drive, dance, or sing....take moments to be alone and gather parts broken... .... stop..... stop this needing you.

Should I hate you? Should I throw rocks at your place or burn you alive? Perhaps...

I should silently walk away to another place... change all there is about me .....And lose myself in this insanity.

1985

Our Day, Thursday

We live for a day, our day, Thursday. The day you belong to me and I
belong to you. Our day, Thursday, we are free to do as we please.

We may linger in bed until late afternoon, holding each other,
kissing, and becoming one.

We may ride the roads for miles and miles in your Mercedes Benz,
as we laugh, talk, and feel the wind blow through our hair.

We enjoy going nowhere planned.

Our day, Thursday, we find comfort in being alone, lost in the
quiet solitude of our private thoughts, where there are no words
needed or spoken.

The closeness we feel; the security we find there in each other's
supportive arms.

Our day, Thursday, a day, a few hours of pleasure, laughter, and fun.

A day for remembering why we are alive in this world.

A day for creating memories for a lifetime.

Still, the day ends and we are left with our good-byes.

We part and the longing begins,

longing for the days and the hours to go quickly …

Until once again,

it's Our day, Thursday

1984

Lonely Seashell

To Hamp

I was one of many until you came along.
You picked me up from the sand and carried me home.
You gently brushed the sand from my weathered skin;
You made me feel... Alive.
I remember how you freely talked to me,
How I found comfort in your soothing words.
Those were the happiest days with you.
Now, I sit here quietly
Listening
For the gentleness of your voice.
Longing to hear your laughter and
The quiet softness of your sleep.
I know your different moods,
When you are happy or when you are feeling blue.
I can taste the salt of your tears when your heart
Has been crying for a love that wasn't true.
If you will come closer...just a little closer,
You will hear my heart is crying too.
I'm just a lonely seashell sitting here on your mantle,
Looking shiny and new, something you
Wanted one day when you were feeling lonely and blue.
Each day that passes I sit here hoping
You will glance my way.

Hoping you will hold and caress me, the way
You did that first day.
Until then, I'll go on remembering
How you chose me over so many,
Took me home, took me in.
A lonely seashell …

1985

Girl

When love begins to fade and your heart turns gray,
Don't be sad, don't get even or mad.
When you find your lover is untrue,
A great pretender of the worst sort,
Stand tall and move swiftly along.
When there is no public display of affection,
You sense subtle changes and see meanness in his actions,
Believe in what is real.
When he looks right through you and speaks
Unkind words meant solely to harm, don't allow
Your mind to grow weary or be tormented.
Remember, you are kinder than he.
When you feel his love has grown faint
And he is barely present,
leave him alone. Move on!
Do not allow your emotions to be played
And your heart left bleeding.
Have courage, and smile. Yes, smile—
For smiles warm the heart and soften the mind.
Smile, for you will be free, free of him.
And remember the day will come
When he will be sorry he is not at your side.
When that day arrives, do not give your heart
A chance to be tried.

Let your intuitive brain take charge,
And leave that fool alone.
Because you have grown into a woman now.
And you will be happy he is gone.

1985

Valentine

To Joey, year of marriage

Your eyes are all I see, no matter where I may be.
Your lips I long to kiss.
Your face I long to caress.
Your love alone I do request.
You are all I cherish; you have touch my heart
and satisfy my soul with your sweet tenderness.
You are all I need—this I do confess.
You are my happiness.

1987

One More Drink

To Will, who lost Karen

What goes through the mind of the man sitting at the bar? He sits there with drink in hand, his thoughts afar, lost from this place—this gloomy place with its dim lights, loud music, nasty floors, and a sassy waitress looking for that extra tip of the day.

His story is the same as many who sit here beside him. It's one more drink, then another. He is drowning his memories, trying to forget the pain, while longing for someone who has gone away.

He sits here quietly with glass in hand, for him there is no future, only the past. He is the image of sadness as he merrily orders one more drink, then another.

The happy hour is over and for him there is a long night ahead. He begins to talk openly to anyone who happens to drop-in. His hand is trembling as he reaches for the bottle, his grip is getting weaker and it's harder to take hold. His vision has become cloudy and he's about to lose control. He thinks of her, his lost love. He believes no one understands his misery, no one but Old Crown. He wants to explain his struggles to anyone who will listen, as he repeats his story, *she was just killing time and pretending to love me … she never loved me … she never did*, one more drink, then another. He lies to himself. He lies to all who will listen. He is determined to drink away his sorrow, *soon she will be gone from my heart, she is gone*, one more drink, then another.

She sits at the bar with drink in hand. She looks in the mirror and reminds herself, I'm just like him; she appreciates the lies he tells because she knows them so well. She has worn those shoes of misery and pain so well. She has walked through those doors in hopes of washing the hurt away, with an ache in her heart and dogged memories that want let her be. She seeks solitude in this bar just like him, one more drink she calls out, then another. For her, it's the gin that helps ease the pain and fade the memories. She raises her glass with a smile and a hello to him, my friend. Together, it's one more drink, then another.

The evening comes to a close. The bartender turns the lights up, pours one more drink for the road. The old man stumbles off the barstool, tips his waitress, and smiles at his neighbor. He's a picture of misery as he makes his way to the door. Slowly, he turns and yells out, "Have one more drink for me!"

1995

Shadowy Path

Do not look for your future down a shadowy path...
Come out of the Forrest...
Look ahead....search, explore, and discover.
Move slowly.... left, right, or make a sharp turn....
The choice is yours
Leave that troubled path... (past)
Filled with darkness, torn branches, and snakes....
Look for the clearing where the sun shines
bright and wild flowers grow....
Breathe easy and smile.
You will make it... I know... because I was there
Not so long ago.

2009

Unforgettable Knowing

LWR, the womanizer

In an instant, that unforgettable knowing happens.
I realized those times of caring, touching, needing
unspoken words of love—
not real,
a well-practiced performance!
My passion, my every heartbeat—
in truth, our epic love affair was your game. A game that ended
suddenly and harshly.
That single moment of knowing
the real you, the undeniable truth of you,
left a soul scarred, a healthy pride diminished, and a heart scorned!
I will journey alone now
with serenity,
a heart intently sealed.
The road beyond is one-way, a mystery to be searched for, explored,
    and somehow enjoyed with eyes wide open.
Regrets securely locked away with precious few memories to think of.
a spirit not afraid to love again—
perhaps
someday.
Still,
The heart knows.
That moment of knowing strengthens or kills.

1995

Never love another

She will never love another. She will never whisper "I love you" to
silent ears.
A heart will forever be sheltered within protective covers far from
harms way, no longer threatened by love's rejection.

Strange how it all seems clear when you realize how weak and foolish
a girl can be, its strangely funny if not painfully comical.

When emotions have control and the brain knows what the heart is
unwilling to accept. She will learn, she will be brave, she will be
smart to know, "never love another."

A detemined heart will battle with the dogged brain and neither will
agree to allow the other to find peace and contentment. The
internal tug of war will agonize the soul.
Even so, a strong heart will continue to beat intently.

A zealous brain will search for new adventures.

A free spirit will forever refuse to lose self.

And she will solemnly vow to "Never love another."

1995

Still

It's daylight.
One is still alive.
A heart is still beating,
beating slow with perfect rhythm.
A body weary from a restless night of mindless turmoil.
Gentle slumber gives little comfort to a tired aching body.
Thoughts, feelings die with the moon's shadow, only to be
brightened by the smiling face of the sun as it peeks
through the windowsill.
The dullness of one's dream is a frown
that comes alive with the
birth of a new day full of clear-blue sunny skies.
Still, still every thought is of you
my friend,
my desire,
my love,
Still.

2001

Cool day

One cool fall day
A heart slowly dying alone
Tenderly aroused...to discover
The sun smiling down onto my face
Butterflies dancing about in my belly
A Passion restored ...alive
Alive! .....and the world is mine
All mine to enjoy!

2001

I Am

"I am," said the face. "Really, I am—I am the person who knows it is difficult indeed and takes a considerable amount of energy to show one face to oneself and another to the multitudes of others. Nonetheless, I must recognize that which is the true face or perhaps I will never know and continue to deceive all … including myself."

2009

Crazy Stupid Weird

You were just one of those crazy, stupid, weird kind of loves that a person must suffer through once in a lifetime.

That feeling of unexplained desire, passion, joy, and misery all wrapped up in one single emotion. One cannot deny the lack of logic. Yet, crazy, stupid, weird kind of love has caused more than a few needy hearts to feel the jaws of rejection.

A bright smile can lose its beauty. An unrequited love then eventually die and that awesome sense of humor will fade, only for a whille. Soon, what began as joyful and fun ends in anger will eventually evolves into a funny reminder of how crazy stupid weird love can be.

One must accept the journey for what it is, …the spring of intense happiness and the winter of emptiness, pain, and regrets.

Yes, the pain will hurt and cause one too whine. Nonetheless, a life without great pain and lots of regrets would be no life at all.

One must experience at least one episode of Crazy, Stupid, Weird kind of love or else live a very boring life with no stories to tell at all!

2009

Once knew a man

To Kush

I once knew a man whose skin was the color of walnut,
Eyes round like saucers, dark as the devil's own soul,
small hands and feet
not so perfect teeth.
He could easily charm you with his innocent childish ways
Betray you with his witty pathetic lies.
A simple mind without reason or abstract thought,
Two-faces, two lives of which others knew naught
Yes it's true. I once thought I knew a man
But no…I did not.

2009

No Tears for Me

In memory of Mom, Dad, siblings
and my sweet Granny Hames

When I die, do not bury me beneath the cold Alabama clay.
No, do not bury me where the insects and bugs play.
Spread me across yonder meadow
Where I can grow and live again one day.
Tell my love that love doesn't die with dying,
That my love lingers in every scent,
Every flower.
In the spring,
Gather all my friends,
Take a slow walk
Down Mallard Creek Road,
Sit quietly
on the bank of the Tennessee River,
Sing "Amazing Grace" and
"Down by the River," say
A little prayer for me—
Jesus and I will hear you.

2009

The Sea

There is something about the sea:
the sounds, the constant movements, the colors,
and its great vastness. The sea with all its wonderments
beckons me to come and explore its emptiness,
discover its hidden treasures, and appreciate its roars.
find inner peace and strength in the unknown
depths of the sea, the magical sea.
Come ride its swift surf, sail its calm waters, or walk its sandy shore—
yet be aware of the ferocious storms with their drenching rains,
high tides, and violent winds as the sea comes alive
for all the world to see. Know
there by the sea, with the wind blowing my hair
and sun warming my cheek—there alone is where I am,
and where I forever will be.

2010

The Wall

My old house in Decatur

The old walls softly whisper to a girl alone in her iron bed...

You are never alone here with me, I'm not like other walls.
I'm strong, structured for endurance, my base is cemented in
concrete, my roof is water proof and will last a lifetime.
You, my sweet girl chose me, saved me from ruin and destruction.
These walls will forever be grateful. You may change my colors,
place nails in my cover, I will not complain! These walls will
listen protectively both day and night for those who would enter
uninvited.
So, sweet girl sleep, sleep quietly in peace. Feel safe...I will be
here when you awake.

2014

The Love of Golf

To Kodani, the lover of Golf

A golf ball.

A golf ball, a wood, or iron club.

A green

A hole in the middle of the green.

A green with a hole in the middle with a flag sticking out, waving
hello to everyone.

The golf ball, the club, the green, the hole, the flag and him.

It's the game of him: the man on the tee, hitting the ball, aiming for
the hole in the green with the flag waving to everyone.

It's the thrill he must feel to know he can enter the hole in less than
par, impress self and others, take the flag and throw it on the
ground, and proudly say "Birdie this one!"

He is sure when the day is done and the trophy is on display that the
next game is only a few short days away.

He is the man who has no other life and plays no other game,

A solitary man who has lost many lovers along the way.

One wonders with interest and somewhat disdain what would make
one love such a game—is it the beauty of the perfectly round
white ball?

Is it the competitive hunger to be superior than other players?

Perhaps the love of golf is simply a personality flaw that no amount
    of wins will satisfy. Nonetheless, one admits the love of golf is
    enjoyable indeed, yet one can easily imagine
The loneliness one would go through if to dare love such a man. She
    will find herself waiting
Behind the ball, the wood, the green, the flag, and the win.

2016

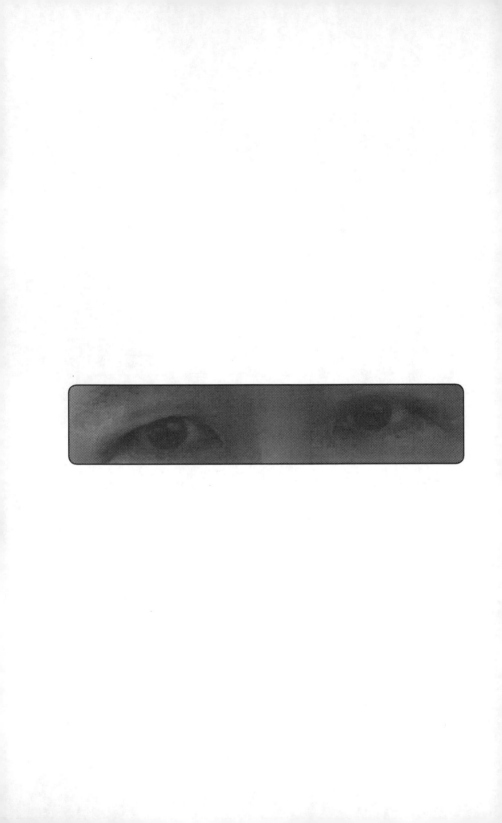

Dark Eyes

To Hiromi, who lost his great love

The room is dark, darker than the coal buried deep in the earth's soil. No light, no light at all in those dark eyes. No light or love, only the darkness of a cold heart.

Her eyes are blue, a deep penetrating blue, like those of the bluebird on yonder windowsill. Blue eyes that can see perfectly within the darkness of his room. She can see those empty dark eyes, eyes that are focused somewhere beyond his silent room, somewhere outside this moment … perhaps yearning for a lost love. Fighting memories that torture a damaged heart and cloud a worried mind.

While he wipes a tear that dampens the corner of his eye, he knows he betrays her. He cannot stop his thoughts, his love for another, so he betrays her while they make love. He tries to hide his emotions, yet his dark eyes tell the story he lacks the courage to speak.

She recalls that it has been famously written that one knows without the telling by the look in a man's eyes if there is real love or truth. It's the unspoken, undoubtable knowing that she sees there in his dark eyes. She declares that his dark eyes tell the entire story vividly, so much so, that the room illuminates with the truthfulness of his dishonesty.

The knowledge seen there in those dark eyes is her reality.

She is determined not to be shattered by the knowing, find comfort in the understanding that the greatest of love most often is lost or not shared.

Still, she cannot forget the man, yet, she vows with solemn conviction that the emptiness seen in his dark eyes will no longer be hers to bear.

2016

Come Softly to Me

Come softly to me. Know me, feel me.
Tell me of your fears, your doubts, your dreams.
Offer yourself to me, hold yourself close to my side. Love me.
Come softly to me. Don't hold back your loving arms.
Let the feelings pour in.

Readily tell me of those feelings you hold dear.
Display for me the passions you hide so effectively
Come softly to me. Be my love.
Come softly to me: teach me the ways to love you.

My heart, my lover, my friend, don't you understand? You cannot
    stop me
from loving you. My heart loves eternally; only when I
exhale my last breath, my heart beats its last beat, will I be silent.
I love you. Even with death beyond this life
I will go on loving you.

Come softly to me:
hear my whispers, feel my soul reaching out from inside my body.
lay your hard head onto my breast, warm my deprived body,
gently caress my lips with your warm moist kisses, light my world
with your tender appraising eyes ... search me, know me!
Come softly to me, dear love;
I am longing for you.
Come softly to me. I am here waiting.

2017

My life… so many changes … all the same
Old lovers-new, painful memories,
mistakes unforgiven, Dreams …
Self-hatred
Lonely nights … brighter days.
A heartbroken…Mended
Shattered, Restored… Again.
One walks alone …. exploring….searching
Rediscovering …..Self

2018

The Truth

To a friend upon her discovering that her husband is gay

She can smell the scent of him, feel his nearness, and see those brown eyes as he stares out at nothing. He is constantly shifting about in bed, moving ever so closer to the edge, afraid to touch, discover, or explore the need in her.

The soft light peeks through the corners of the door and the reflection of his quiet face indicates agony, lack of desire, and deep emptiness. She is aware and feels the inner turmoil that is hidden there.

She knows.

She begs for honest words to be spoken.

For the truth of us, our marriage.

Yet, it is he, the quiet self-absorbed man who lies awake in the darkness of this cold dark room, unable to speak or sleep. It is he, who has no emotional care for her, a heart that is true. It is he, whose thoughts and feelings are wide open for her to read like large print on a canvas.

It is he, who knows the truth of their marriage, yet will not speak.

2020

Sally Was Never My Name

To Mary, My Mother

She is awake, dreading the sound of that old Ford pickup truck as it pulls up in the driveway. It's getting close to three in the morning and she knows it's his usual quitting time. He will leave the whiskey, poker, and friends to make his way home to his wife and children.

The calm stillness of the cool night air consoles her for a few hours, yet she is aware of what is coming. She lies awake in bed tossing and turning with anticipation. The insomnia is worse than usual as she turns once more. She quietly whispers, *I need rest*, clinging her hands together as she takes a deep breath with dread. She prays for sleep, if only for a few minutes, but no sleep—for she hears the sound of that old Ford pickup truck pulling up into the driveway.

The sound is so familiar and the fear never goes away. The sounds of the tires on the gravel road, that old muffler whining as the motor slowly turns off, the slamming of the truck door. The squeaking of the old screen door as he opens it and walks in. She recognizes his staggering footsteps on the wood floor and the quick flash of light as he opens the bedroom door. *O Lord*, she prays, *Please, make it quick and easy.*

He hangs his shirt and pants on the bedpost, pulls back the covers, and slips between the sheets as he whispers, "Sally, are you awake?" His hands feel cold and awkward although she has felt his touch a thousand times before. Again he whispers, "Sally, Sally, are you ready?" as he enters her secret place. "Sally, I'll only be a minute. Sally, you feel good to me as always."

She lies quietly and listens to his whispers, his moans, and feels his touch. She cries inward knowing it would be useless to object out loud. She turns on her side and faces the wall and sees herself vaguely in the distant mirror. She is relieved that it's all over and she can rest for a while. She does not say a word, hides her tears as he slowly moves away to the other side of the bed. He says, "Sally, wake me up in a few hours" as he turns farther away.

She lies there thinking, *Why, why? After nine kids and twenty years of marriage. Why you call me Sally, why you call me Sally? Sally was never my name.*

Shortly she hears the rhythm of his snoring. It's getting louder and she is thankful he can do no more harm tonight. He is content and sleeping soundly, while she turns moving farther off to her side of the bed, wiping tears from her eyes as she says a silent prayer to Jesus: *Please don't let there be another child. Please, Lord, I cannot bear one more.*

After nine kids and twenty years of marriage, why you call me Sally? Why you call me Sally? Sally was never my name.

2022

No Love At All

To a friend, divorcing a real jerk

She thought her love would be eternal because she loved him just yesterday.

How, in a moment of knowing she must acknowledge there was no love at all.

The coolness of his touch, the darkness of his eyes, no laughter or feeling of emotional ties.

An unfriendly breakup and a cold goodbye.

Perhaps the spark of love has finally died! A girl will never know the reason or seek to understand why. Yet, she can easily read between the lines and comprehend the unspoken words that are written there in his eyes.

He may not give a damn how he makes her feel. But, giving time, he will come to realize the harm he has caused a loving heart will not be ever-lasting.

She will over-come loves rejection and move forward pitying the man who lacks passion, adventure, and courage to be true to love.

She will remember and most likely never forget

A man who has

No love at all.

2022

Surgery

Ramblings of a patient after open heart surgery

I woke up this morning with the most awful hurting in my chest, it felt like someone was stabbing me to death. The pain jolted me awake! I felt this odd device wedged in my throat, I was gagging. I began tossing and turning my head back and forth. Oh no, I thought!

Am I about to choke to death.

Then, my brain began to think rationally and I understood, I have been in surgery. I was intubated and this tube in my throat is allowing air into my lungs. Oh damn, I forget the need for air, as crazy thoughts keep running through my head. Should I pull the damn thing out, reaching for the tube, I realize, *my hands are tied?*

Somewhere I could hear a voice telling me be calm, be happy, feel joyful.

Feel joyful! Your old tired heart has kept right on beating, and you are alive. The voice quickly vanished, the joy was short-lived and soon totally forgotten.

The most excruciating pain shot through my chest. *Oh God, this pain in my chest is killing me, someone please help!*

I was straining trying to see what was this weight on my chest. *tubes, wires, and more wires attached to my breast and chest.* I noticed.

The constant beep, beep, beep sounded strange ringing in my ears, damn, damn, damn the noise is aggravating me to the point of craziness. I struggled to free my bound hands…No use, *I'm a prisoner here.*

My eyes scanned the room and focused on my son sitting across the way in a visitor's chair. I could see my reflection through his teary eyes. The helpless look I saw there made me attempt to hide the excruciating pain I was feeling. I swore to myself, I will not cry out loud or shed any tears, I will not. But lord, *I've never hurt this bad before.*

The noise in the room was getting louder, what is the problem with all these people making so much noise? *I asked myself.* My head is hurting, feels like drumbeats pounding in my head. *Please stop the alarms, voices, and all the walking about in this room,*

I screamed to myself. *What can I do? No one seems to understand.* I pulled at my bound wrists once more as I prayed for mercy. *Does anyone see I'm in agony here?*

It's evening now, my senses are on overload. Even the gentle touch of my daughter's hand intensifies the pain*, oh how I wish I was dead.*

I'm lying in this miserable bed with wild thoughts running through my head.

I am alive, I have survived the knife, but then again, *I really don't give a damn.* I am awake and aware, *the worst is yet to come.* I must get up out of this bed, and once again I think, *the worst is yet to come.* With every breath, my chest is killing me.

Lord, Lord, this hurting in my chest is killing me.

September, 28, 2022

Longing for Nothing at All

As she travels down a familiar highway, the reflection in the hazy rearview mirror is unrecognizable. The watery blue eyes are empty and blink every so often. Her perfectly round face is pale and hidden of emotion. *Who is this person looking back at me? Looking through me, seeing my very soul?* As she travels, she is quiet, her thoughts are obscured yet, deep inside her she has a gut feeling of knowing that which she cannot control.

She feels an emptiness not easily recognized or described.

The heart flutters faintly in her chest. There is an awareness of her state of mind that leaves her with a feeling of giddiness and loss of control. Memories overwhelm her thoughts, and those blue eyes weep, weep tears of pain.

Why, why? Again she cries, *Why?*

As she rides along the familiar highway, glancing every so often into the hazy mirror, she faces the reality of knowing that which her lover knew from the beginning: it was fun for him, a regrettable love for her.

Lost, nowhere to find comfort, silent and fighting her inner emotions, driving the long familiar highway and longing for nothing …

Longing for nothing at all.

July 2022

Reflections
and
Old Sayings

You know a friend by their
actions in front of others.

You know it's not love by
their ability to hurt you badly
without a second thought.

(how I felt when my first real love dumped me for an ugly woman
he had been dating for years, named Patsy)

Your brain knows what
your heart will hide.

When your heart bleeds
enough it will listen most
carefully to the brain.

No flaccid penis can satisfy.

He did not satisfy the soul but,
the heart loved him anyway.

One who smiles at strangers with a quirky hello is fake to the bone!

(an old acquaintance would always change her accent and tone of voice when she was introduced to anyone she thought had money or clout, funny!)

He can kiss my ass and
bark at the anal hole.

(an old expression my grandma would say, except she left out the
anal)

"Love you more" flippant phrase?

(real or just a rehearsed meaningless phrase)

Love does not die with dying; love lives in the spirit and ascends into heaven full of much happiness.

(you know love never dies when you lose a parent, child, sibling, or partner. love is always alive)

You can marry more in a minute
than you can earn in a lifetime.

(excellent advice from my mother, as usual I did not heed)

If you do not love, sooner or later even their breathing will annoy you.

(learning that you must love a person to stay with them, or else suffer in silence to their snoring)

If you did not document,
it was not done.

(a nursing saying, that I thought must be printed again)

You are only as good as your
word and words must have
actions to mean anything.

If he/she is debating whether this one or that one is the right choice....run like hell Genuine feelings are not a check off list of what fits, that is called shopping.

I had this most wonderful feeling that I knew you, a mindless heart felt notion that you were the one for me….wrong!

We are standing on a cliff waiting for something wonderful to happen, hoping that it will be something wonderful. (I read the book "Something Wonderful" by Judith McNaught, a similar phrase was in the book, I too believe that we are all in some way waiting for something wonderful).

A man who loves you will never give you a reason to cry.

The key that opens the door to a new beginning is: doing silly things, laughing out loud often, listen to music that touches your soul, dance alone, writing poems to expose naked self, and cry until tears taste sweet.

Life goes full circle. You are born and you die...All that comes in between can be considered fate, luck and self- determination. You grow, you learn, you laugh, you play, you cry and sometimes you fail. You feel love and love can be wonderful or love can break you.

The days, months, years rush by and before you blink twice a life has flown by. With age time is the center focus of your thoughts. Do I have time? Time left for goals? Time to fulfill desires? Time to meet challenges? Time to change and start again. TIME... time will eventually threaten your existence and slowly vanish your hopes. Suddenly, self-preservation will become the primary need, a place of calm resolve. Change and acceptance becomes interchangeable. Death is looming, family and friends die while memories remain alive. A career ends and the unique self is found. Love is ever-lasting, life ends and eternal life begins.

Printed in the United States
by Baker & Taylor Publisher Services